U0065799

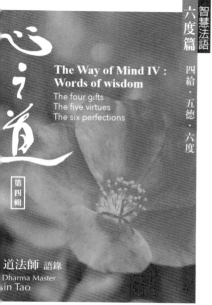

智慧法語

六度篇

四給・五德・六度

心之道

The Way of Mind IV :
Words of wisdom

The four gifts
The five virtues
The six perfections

第四輯

道法師 語錄
Dharma Master
in Tao

目錄

Contents

The four gifts :
joy, confidence, hope, and skillful means
The five virtues :
positive attitude, zeal, optimism, love,
and the power of a vow
The six perfections :
generosity, morality, patience, energy,
concentration, and wisdom

　　心道法師一九四八
年生，祖籍雲南，幼失
依怙，為滇緬邊境孤
雛。十三歲隨孤軍撤
移來台，十五歲初聞觀
音菩薩聖號，有感於觀
音菩薩的悲願，以「悟
性報觀音」、「吾不成
佛誓不休」、「真如度
眾生」刺身供佛，立誓

徹悟真理，救度苦難。

　　二十五歲出家後，頭陀行腳歷十餘年，前後在台北外雙溪、宜蘭礁溪圓明寺、蒴仔崙墳塔、龍潭公墓和員山周舉人廢墟，體驗世間最幽隱不堪的「塚間修」，矢志修證，了脫生死，覺悟本來。

無生道場」，展開弘法
度生的佛行事業，為現
代人擘劃成佛地圖。為
了推動宗教共存共榮，
法師以慈悲的華嚴理念
奔走國際，並於二〇〇
一年十一月成立世界宗
教博物館，致力於各種
不同宗教的對話，提昇
對所有宗教的寬容、尊

規範;「般若期」著重
在明瞭與貫徹空性智
慧;「法華期」著重生
起願力,發菩提心;
「華嚴期」則強調多元
共存、和諧共生,證
入圓滿無礙的境界。

　　近年來,心道法
師以「一心到六度」六
項生活原則,作為普羅

人方便;「五德」正
面、積極、樂觀、愛
心、願力;「六度」
布施、持戒、忍辱、
精進、禪定、智慧。

　　心道法師以禪的
攝心觀照為本、教育
弘法為主軸,用慈悲
願力守護人類心靈,
以世界和平為終生職

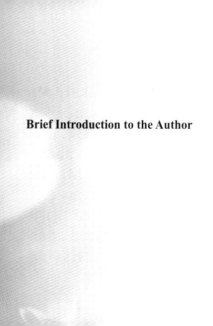

Brief Introduction to the Author

Born in upper Myanmar in 1948 to ethnic Chinese parents of Yunnan Province, Master Hsin Tao was left orphaned and impoverished at an early age. Having been taken in by the remnants of ROC military units operating along the border of Yunnan, China, he was brought to Taiwan in 1961 when he was 13. At the age of 15, he

As an offering to
the Buddha, he had
himself tattooed
with the vows
"May I awaken
in gratitude for
the kindness of
Guanyin,""I will
never rest until

Buddhahood is attained, "and "Liberating all beings by living from the core of one's being."

After becoming a Buddhist monk at the age of 25

locations, including Waishuangxi in Taipei, Yuanming Temple in Yilan, Chingtzulun Grave Tower, Longtan Cemetery, and the ruins of the frist-degree Scholar Chou

during which time
he attained deep
insight into the
meaning of "Only
when all beings
are liberated, is
enlightenment fully
attained." Standing
on the summit of the

Ling Jiou Mountain, looking down at the Pacific Ocean, Master Hsin Tao felt great compassion for the suffering of all sentient beings. After his solitary retreat he established

world a proper path
to enlightenment.
In addition,
Master Hsin Tao
strived hard to
gain international
support with the
compassionate spirit
of the Buddhist

the construction
of the Museum of
World Religions in
November 2001.
This Museum
is dedicated to
advancing the cause
of world peace
and a promoting

approach applicable to both monastics and lay practitioners alike to help them deepen their practice. Frist comes the āgama stage, which centers on the foundational teachings of Buddhism and the three-fold practice of morality, concentration, and wisdom. The Prajñā stage emphasizes the insight into and practice of

Master Hsin Tao has been encouraging his disciples to apply the "six principles of spiritual practice" in their daily lives, as a way of implementing his teaching that "Work

acts of goodness are
wholesome actions
of body, speech,
and mind. The
four gifts are joy,
confidence, hope,
and skillful means.
The five virtues:
positive attitude,

has devoted himself to propagating the Dharma through education, based on the Chan principle of concentrating the mind and seeing one's original Buddha-nature. Through compassion, he makes great efforts to protect and care for all sentient beings. Taking the establishment of world peace as his lifelong

The Way of Mind IV : Words of wisdom
The four gifts / The five virtues / The six perfections
智慧法語
六度篇

through Dharma
p r a c t i c e   f o r
generations to come.

六度篇 ——

四給： 給人歡喜、給人信心、
給人希望、給人方便

五德： 正面、積極、樂觀、
愛心、願力

六度： 布施、持戒、忍辱、
精進、禪定、智慧

The Six Perfections ——

The four gifts :
joy, confidence, hope, and skillful means

The five virtues :
positive attitude, zeal, optimism, love,
and the power of a vow

The six perfections :
generosity, morality, patience, energy,
concentration, and wisdom

四給—給人歡喜、
信心、希望、方便，
是我們修行的工具。

The four gifts—joy,
confidence, hope, and
skillful means—can be
seen as tools for spiritual
practice.

把身、口、意三好做好，
就能給人歡喜、信心、
希望、方便。

By being established in wholesome actions of body, speech, and mind, we are able to give others the four gifts—joy, confidence, hope, and skillful means.

Giving the four gifts
benefits others and carries
us along the path of
buddhahood.

Take every opportunity
to share the
Buddha's teaching;
maintain the heart of
kindness and compassion.

多讚美、多鼓勵，
讓人找到
生命最美好的一面。

Make an effort to encourage
others to find the beauty
in life.

諸惡莫作、
眾善奉行，
用佛法淨化人心。

Refrain from all evil;
engage in every type
of goodness;
use the Buddha's teaching
to purify the mind and
heart.

Truly benefiting others
begins with letting go of
selfish motivations.

Wholesome affinities bring
all virtues and undertakings
to completion.

順緣、善緣做多，
障礙就少。

The more the
wholesome affinities,
the less the obstacles.

Maintain continual
awareness and universal
compassion.

三好是學修養，
四給是學領導，
五德是結好緣。

The three acts of goodness
are a form of self-cultivation;
the four gifts are a form
of leadership;
the five virtues are for
establishing positive
affinities.

五德就是
正面、積極、樂觀、
愛心、願力。

The five virtues: positive attitude, zeal, optimism, love, and the power of a vow.

所有一切都是流動的，
只有慈悲心和覺醒的心
才是自己可以主宰的。

The Way of Mind IV : Words of wisdom
The four gifts / The five virtues / The six perfections
智慧法語
六度篇

In a world of constant flux,
the only things that can be
truly controlled are your
own compassion
and awareness.

生從因果來，
死也從因果去。
我們把因做好，
就可以創造我們的好命。

Both birth and death are subject to the law of cause and effect; establishing good causes brings good fortune.

傳承佛法、利益眾生，
增長我們生命中的富貴。

Propagating the Buddha's teaching for the benefit of all sentient beings brings good fortune.

佛法就像眼睛，
帶你開拓
正面、積極、
樂觀、大愛的生命。

The Buddha's teaching
is what guides us in the
development of a
positive attitude, zeal,
optimism, love,
and the power of a vow.

Practicing Buddhism is a
way of managing one's life
so that it becomes more
positive and fulfilling.

Engaging in
wholesome deeds generates
positive energy.

正面就是正能量，
能使人快樂、歡喜。

Maintaining a positive attitude brings energy, joy, and happiness.

只要你是正面積極的，
你的朋友、家庭
也會是正面、積極的。

When you have a positive
attitude and zeal it rubs off
on all those around you.

Negativity is the bane of success.

保持樂觀，
隨時給人喜悅。

在生活中，
用佛法將所有的煩憂
轉換成隨喜功德。

The Buddha's teaching
shows us how to transform
negativity into rejoicing
in the virtue of others.

Loving kindness is a form of concern for others which generates good karma.

A loving heart generates happiness.

當你有愛心，
就會覺得生命是
多麼的有力量，
一切的動力
都從愛心而來。

When the heart is
filled with love,
we feel energized;
love is a powerful
motive force.

愛心是生命中的陽光，
我們有愛心，
人生就是彩色的。

A loving heart fills life with
sunshine and color.

愛心是
生命中的潤滑油，
生命中的快樂
都是從愛心來的。

Love is the lubricant of
life and the source of all
happiness.

有愛心才會有願力，
有願力就會去完成
所有慈悲的工作。

Only when the heart is filled
with love is it possible to
make a vow of compassion
and bring it to fulfillment.

Compassion is the
application of
wholesome vows.

學佛要有願力，
落實正見的生活。

To practice Buddhism you need the power of a vow and a way of life guided by right views.

Without the power of a
vow, you lack a clear sense
of purpose and direction.

生命要有願力，
對家庭和社會做出貢獻。

With the power of a vow,
we can make a positive
contribution to our family
and society.

眾生是我們佛國淨土
的一個願力。

Our inspiration to be reborn
in the pure land comes from
all sentient beings.

So long as sentient beings
continue to suffer, our vow
of compassion remains
unfulfilled.

我們要學習用大願力、
大慈悲、大智慧
來成就佛國淨土。

Bringing a pure land to completion requires universal compassion, great wisdom, and the power of a vow.

The power of a vow arises
from insight into life.

六度就是
布施、持戒、忍辱、
精進、禪定、智慧。

The six perfections are
generosity, morality,
patience, energy,
concentration,
and wisdom.

六度是度自己，
讓我們精進地生活。

The six perfections are tools
for spiritual development;
they invest your life with
energy.

Cultivating the six
perfections gives rise to
unobstructed wisdom.

布施就是給予、能捨，
除去執著的方法。

捨就是奉獻與服務，
從捨裡面把心放下。

Donating your time and
resources helps you let go
of self-centeredness.

Let your heart and mind
always be filled with
generosity, compassion,
and wisdom.

By practicing generosity
we accumulate positive
affinities.

我們要能夠
貢獻、服務，
給的生命是最富足的。

Prosperity comes from
giving and serving others.

要自度度他
就是要布施，
然後從布施裡面
得到善緣。

The Way of Mind IV : Words of wisdom
The four gifts / The five virtues / The six perfections
智慧法語
六度篇

Generosity is necessary for
the salvation of oneself
and others;
it's also a way of
establishing positive
affinities.

布施加無我，
才有空性的力量。

Generosity augmented with selflessness generates the power of emptiness.

不起心、不動念、
不攀緣的心，
就叫做持戒。

The uncluttered mind
free of thoughts and
attachments—this is what's
called morality.

Upholding the precepts is a way of refining the mind by filtering out all the crude mental habits characteristic of the untrained mind, making it possible to cultivate deep insight in meditation.

A life of morality is a happy life.

A life guided by precepts
is a life without regret.

戒就是自我約束，
能夠不傷害別人，
自己又獲得利益。

Endowed with morality
and self-restraint,
you benefit yourself and
refrain from harming
others.

在布施和持戒上
不斷地精進，
是善業的一種法則。

Striving forward endowed
with generosity and
precepts, good karma
follows as a matter of
course.

從戒裡規矩生活，
從定裡不攀緣，
從慧裡照見諸法空相。

Precepts bring an orderly life; concentration tames the clambering mind; wisdom reveals the emptiness of all conditioned things.

Patience is a bridge leading
to abundant happiness.

安忍在
一切諸法正見上，
回到
一切寂靜不變的地方，
也就是回到
空性的本質。

Patiently abiding in the
right view of all things,
we return to the place of
unchanging silence,
the essence of emptiness.

The Way of Mind IV : Words of wisdom
The four gifts / The five virtues / The six perfections
六度篇
智慧法語

Quietly abide in the
nature of the mind;
diligently cultivate patience
in all situations.

Energy is necessary for the continual contemplation of emptiness.

A scattered mind
depletes our energy;
chanting a mantra
replenishes our energy.

人身難得，
努力精進學習與修行。

A human rebirth is
hard to attain;
make the most of it by
fully applying yourself to
spiritual cultivation.

想法清淨就是戒，
安住不躁動就是忍，
持續地淨念相續
就是精進。

Morality is purity of mind; patience is calmly abiding; energy is perseverance in purifying the mind.

禪修
就是找回自己那份
不生不滅的靈知靈覺。

Chan meditation is a way
of returning to that spiritual
awareness that neither
arises nor ceases.

禪修，
沒有過去、現在、未來，
只有當下這一念。

In Chan meditation there is
no past, no present,
no future;
only the present moment
exists.

持戒和禪定，
讓心不再流浪。

Precepts and concentration
reign in the desultory mind.

Concentration tames the
heart and mind and sets the
stage for the arising
of wisdom.

Remaining firmly settled in emptiness and continually contemplating its nature—this is meditative concentration.

Use meditation to
understand emptiness;
use it to return to yourself.

Quietly abiding in your
original face,
you arrive at the
stillness of emptiness.

用無我
去實踐利他的慈悲。

Use selfless compassion to
benefit others.

Compassion means
benefitting others;
meditation means
benefitting oneself.

禪的世界內在無爭、
平靜柔軟而慈悲。

The inner world of Chan
meditation is characterized
by tranquility, compassion,
and litheness of mind.

禪坐可以調伏自心，
把有的心化作無，
無的心化作慈悲。

In Chan meditation we learn how to settle our heart, how to transform existence into non-existence, and non-existence into compassion.

從禪修去明白，
從慈悲去放下所有的
念頭跟執著。

Use meditation to
cultivate insight;
use compassion to let go of
all notions and attachments.

覺醒的生活，
就是用智慧來面對
無常的變化。

A life of awakening means
using wisdom to understand
and face impermanence.

所謂的智慧
就是我們的覺醒，
覺醒就是不迷失在
貪、瞋、癡的習氣裡。

Wisdom means awakening.
Endowed with wisdom,
we no longer get fooled by
our habitual greed, hatred,
and delusion.

Clear comprehension of all things and the ability to distinguish between right and wrong—this is wisdom.

Wisdom is like a sun which
illuminates both body
and mind.

Wisdom is what brings
unimpeded understanding.

Benefitting all sentient
beings requires
both wisdom and
power of action.

智慧就是讓我們
消融煩惱，
知道怎麼去把善業做好，
遠離一切惡緣。

Wisdom dissolves
the defilements;
it shows us how to engage
in skillful actions and
refrain from unskillful
actions.

隨身智慧寶典

心之道

智慧法語系列①~④輯

閱讀心道法師語錄，
可以讓個人在日常生活中如實觀照；
一天一法語，啓開智慧「心」生活。

The Way of Mind I~IV:
Words of wisdom

心道法師 語錄
By Dharma Master
Hsin Tao

靈鷲山般若書坊

第一輯

修慧篇 Cultivate Wisdom

修心篇 Cultivate Mind

修行篇 Cultivate Spirituality

第二輯

Compassion 慈悲篇

Joyful Giving 喜捨篇

第三輯

律己篇 Self-restraint

止觀篇 Tranquility and insight

願力篇 The force of a vow

證果篇 Realization

第四輯

One Heart, One Mind 一心篇

The Six Perfections 六度篇

心之道智慧法語 第四輯

六度篇——四給／五德／六度

心道法師語錄

總 策 劃：釋了意
主 編：洪淑妍
責任編輯：林美伶
英文翻譯：甘修慧
英文審校：Dr. Maria Reis Habito
美術設計：黃偉哲
發 行 人：黃如汝
出版發行：財團法人靈鷲山般若文教基金會附設出版社
劃撥戶名：財團法人靈鷲山般若文教基金會附設出版社
劃撥帳號：18887793
地　　址：23444 新北市永和區保生路2號21樓
電　　話：(02) 2232-1008
傳　　真：(02) 2232-1010
網　　址：www.093books.com.tw
讀者信箱：books@ljm.org.tw
法律顧問：永然聯合法律事務所
印　　刷：東豪印刷事業有限公司
初版一刷：2018年8月
定　　價：新台幣220元（1套2冊）
I S B N：978-986-96539-3-0
總 經 銷：飛鴻國際行銷股份有限公司

The Way of Mind IV : Words of wisdom
The Six Perfections ——The four gifts / The five virtues / The six perfections

Words of Dharma Master Hsin Tao

General Planer : Ven.Liao Yi Shih
Editor in Chief : Hung, Shu-yen
Editor in Charge : Lin, Mei-ling
English translator : Ken Kraynak
English Proofreading : Dr. Maria Reis Habito
Art Editor : Huang, Wei-jer
Publisher : Huang, Hung-ju
Published by and The postal service is allocated :
Ling Jiou Mountain Press, Ling Jiou Mountain Prajna
Cultural and Educational Foundation
Account number : 18887793
Address : 21F., No.2, Baosheng Rd., Yonghe Dist., New
Taipei City 23444, Taiwan (R.O.C.)
Tel : (02)2232-1008 / Fax : (02)2232-1010
Website : www.093books.com.tw
E-mail : books@ljm.org.tw
Legal Consultant : Y. R. Lee & Partners Attorneys at Law
Printing : Sunrise Printing Co., Ltd.
The First Printing of the First Edition : August, 2018
List Price : NT$ 220 dollars (Two-Manual Set)
ISBN :978-986-96539-3-0
Distributor : Flying Horn International Marketing Co., Ltd.

國家圖書館出版品預行編目(CIP)資料

心之道智慧法語.第四輯 / 洪淑妍主編.-- 初版.
-- 新北市：靈鷲山般若出版, 2018. 08
冊 ； 公分
ISBN 978-986-96539-3-0 (全套：精裝)

1. 佛教說法　2. 佛教教化法

225. 4　　　　　　　　　　　　　107011669